CW00920579

Art Activities

That are easy to prepare and that children will love

Paula Goodridge

Brilliant
PUBLICATIONS

Other titles in the 100+ Fun Ideas series:

This book is dedicated to Mrs Louise Strachan, teacher at Andoversford Primary School, Gloucestershire, for her allowing me to help with her After-School Years 5–6 Art Club and for the fun we had in the process!

Published by Brilliant Publications
Unit 10, Sparrow Hall Farm
Edlesborough, Dunstable
Bedfordshire, LU6 2ES, UK
www.brilliantpublications.co.uk

Sales and stock enquiries:
Tel: 01202 712910
Fax: 0845 1309300
E-mail: brilliant@bebc.co.uk
General information enquiries:
Tel: 01525 222292

The name Brilliant Publications and the logo are registered trademarks.

Written by Paula Goodridge
Illustrated by Michelle Ives

© Text Paula Goodridge 2009
© Design Brilliant Publications 2009

ISBN 978-1-905780-33-4

First printed and published in the UK in 2009

The right of Paula Goodridge to be identified as the author of this work has been asserted by herself in accordance with the Copyright, Designs and Patents Act 1988.

Contents

Art Activities

Introduction

The aim of this book is to provide ideas for art activities that teachers can use in the classroom, parents/carers can use at home, or that can be used in children's clubs. The activities are a fun way for children to learn about art, and they are easy to prepare. They are fully compatible with the National Curriculum.

All ideas have been used in a Key Stage 2 classroom, where groups of children have also enjoyed helping with the preparation of some lessons, under supervision. Most enjoy helping with the clearing away afterwards, especially if they gain a small reward! (See award certificate on page 121.)

Although aimed at the Key Stage 2 age group, the ideas could be used for younger children, adapting the activities to suit abilities.

The majority of activities may be used for a whole-class lesson; others are best done in smaller groups, depending on the facilities of your room.

Useful tips

Resources

I have listed resources needed for each activity so you can see at a glance which things will be needed. Below I have listed some extra ideas for obtaining resources, which I have found invaluable in the past, especially if teaching art in the long term.

✦ Picture bank – It is of huge use to keep a constant look out for pictures from sources like magazines, the Internet and postcards. Cut these out and back them on cardboard, and sort them into themes such as: buildings, faces, plants, flowers, transport and artists' work. If you can laminate them, the pictures will last longer. Pictures act as a great stimulus for children, and once you have built up this resource bank, preparation time will be lessened. You may choose to store these centrally, and involve your colleagues in collecting pictures that you can all use.

✦ Internet – An excellent resource for finding pictures and information on artists, cultures and religious artefacts.

✦ Visitors – Many county councils will have a list of working artists who may be willing to come in and do an art activity for your class. You may have to pay for this, but children tend to benefit greatly from meeting a 'real-life' artist. Other visitors, such as art students and historical experts, may also be used as a 'human stimulus' for learning in art, but ensure that they have the appropriate checks for working with children.

✦ Libraries, art galleries and museums – Librarians and curators of galleries and museums are usually very helpful in providing support with resources or information, so too are tourist information centres and historical/religious societies. Key

Stage 2 children could write letters to local sources of interest, so that you may gather resources for a particular topic. Again, this saves your preparation time. The Internet, again, is a good way of finding contact details for these organizations.

✦   Teaching centre – Your local teacher support centre may have boxes of artefacts or packs of pictures on a specific theme that you can borrow for a period of time. By making just one telephone call or filling in one form, you gain a whole new resource box for your children!

✦   Scrap stores and local businesses – In some areas you can find scrap stores or recycling centres that may let you have resources for free, or for a minimal cost. Local businesses such as printing firms or fabric shops may donate cardboard from packaging or fabric remnants.

✦   Parents/Carers – Ask the parents/guardians of your pupils if they have any materials like fabric, wool or buttons that they could donate to an art project.

Children's ideas book

I've found it very useful to provide the children, at the start of the year, with an art book or folder into which they could put down their ideas. They can do rough sketches, try out shading with various pencils or simply stick in pictures that they like. The book is also useful to take outside, should you wish to do some observational drawing in a nature area or at a local historical building. As they have this book in constant use, your preparation time is lowered again, as you are not always searching for paper for planning work.

Paint tips

✦   Liquid paints come in all colours, but better results can often be seen when the children mix their own colours. Sometimes just give the children red, yellow and blue, and get them to produce their own colours from these three. KS2 are very capable of doing this and find it very rewarding. They learn much more about colour mixing in this way.

◆ If you are using shades avoid black; give them white and ask them to add small amounts of one colour to it gradually.

◆ Texture can be changed by adding other materials to paint. For example, experiment by adding flour, sand or PVA glue to paint. Use thick paint for one activity, and then use watery paint for another.

◆ Using limited colours can also be very effective. If, for example, you are studying African art, limit the colours to oranges, browns and reds, or get the children to choose just three colours when producing a pattern. Ask the children what is effective about limiting the colours at the end of your session. Above all, experiment!

Paper ideas

◆ Try to vary the materials the children use. For example, do not always give white A4 paper to the children; change the colour, size or texture of the paper.

◆ Why give them rectangular paper all the time? Why not give them a square or a circle on which to produce their artwork? Could they paint on fabric as opposed to paper? Could they paint or draw on a 3D object first covered in paper? You can also vary the type of pencil, size of brush or clay tools that they may use.

Keeping the children and room tidy

It is a good idea to ask the children to bring in old shirts for use as art aprons, for the more messy activities. Covering all surfaces with old newspapers will help to making tidying up easier.

1. **Runner beans**

You will need: sketching pencils; runner beans; pale green sugar paper; chalks.

✦ Give each child a runner bean, and ask them to really look at it.

✦ Do they see different shades of green? Are there any other colours or markings? What does the bean feel like? What is it shaped like?

✦ Give them each a long, thin rectangle of pale green sugar paper and a sketching pencil. Ask them to lightly sketch their runner bean, filling up as much of the paper as they can.

✦ Once they are happy with their sketch, get them to colour in their beans, using shades of green and possibly brown chalks.

✦ By using white chalk and smudging the white into the greens, they can obtain varying shades.

✦ To get the beans to appear 3D, ask the children to look at dark and light shades on their bean. By shading darker patches the bean will appear fuller instead of flat.

2. **Sweetcorn**

You will need: sketching pencils; brown sugar paper; sweetcorn (ideally one for each child); oil pastels; thin charcoal.

✦ Look very carefully at some sweetcorn.

✦ As with the runner-bean activity, ask the children about the colours or the shades that they see as well as markings and patterns.

✦ How can they make the sweetcorn look round, not flat?

✦ Give them each a rectangle of brown sugar paper, and ask them to sketch their sweetcorn.

✦ When they are happy, ask them to colour in their sweetcorn using oil pastels. Oil pastels do not smudge, like chalk, so pupils will need to vary the pressure to get different shades of colour.

✦ Use the charcoal after they have used the oils, to outline the sweetcorn and to go over any patterning that they wish to stand out.

✦ Other vegetables may be used for the above, but sweetcorn always seems to produce good results!

3. Fruit

You will need: pictures of fruit by various artists; pencils; chalks and pastels; sugar paper; various fruits.

✦ Show the pictures to your group and discuss what they see.

✦ Explain that we use the term 'still life' to describe a work of art depicting mostly inanimate subject matter. They can either be of natural items (eg food, plants, stones or shells) or man-made items (eg vases, coins, artefacts, etc).

✦ Ask the children to each choose one of the fruits you have brought, and ask them to draw it.

✦ They may choose to colour it using chalks, chalk pastels or oil-based pastels.

✦ Create a picture of a large bowl and place all of the children's fruit drawings in it as a collaborative 'still life' art display. You could add some fruit pictures by famous artists, together with some comments on the pictures written by the children themselves.

4. Shoes

You will need: paper; shoes; sketching pencils; charcoals.

✦ Ask the children to take off one of their shoes and place it in front of them.

✦ Get them to observe patterns, markings and shapes.

✦ Give them paper and a sketching pencil, and ask them to lightly sketch their shoe.

✦ Go over the lines of the drawing using charcoals, and use a finger to smudge the charcoal to obtain various shades.

5. Old buildings (1)

You will need: sketching pencils; sketch books; possibly extra adult support, depending on your location.

✦ Give each child a sketching pencil and take them outside with their sketch books to an old building such as a church, mosque or castle (preferably a building over 100 years old).

✦ Make sketches of the whole building or 'zoom in' and make several sketches of just one part of it, for example a spire, cupola or turret.

✦ When you return, discuss what they liked or noticed about the building, and what told them that it was old. Is the age reflected in their drawings?

6. Old buildings (2)

You will need: a jug of cooled coffee; white paper; brushes; black and brown colouring pencils; sketching pencils.

✦ Each child will need to brush the cold coffee over a sheet of white paper, which will make it look old when it's completely dry. (Use paper without a shine on it, as shiny paper absorbs less liquid.)

✦ When the paper is dry, ask the children to choose their best sketch from the previous activity and to redraw it neatly onto the 'old-style paper', using a sketching pencil.

✦ Then fill in the sketches using only brown and black colouring pencils. Press harder to obtain darker shades and put less pressure on the pencils to obtain lighter shades. The black can also be used to outline the sketch, too.

✦ Display the children's sketches with some pictures of old buildings and perhaps some writing by the children on 'how they can tell the building is old'.

7. Modern buildings

You will need: pictures of modern buildings; pictures of abstract buildings by various artists; coloured pencils; A5 paper.

✦ Give each child, or pair of children, a picture of a modern building that is less than 50 years old, and discuss what makes the buildings look new. You could compare them to the old buildings they have sketched previously.

✦ Next, as a whole class, show them some pictures of buildings done by artists who have used an abstract approach, and discuss what they see.

✦ Give them paper and pencils and ask them to create their own modern building, using an abstract style of their own.

8. **Out of a window**

You will need: sketching pencils; A4 white paper; A4 brown or black sugar paper; pencils or pastels of your choice; scissors.

◆ Ask the children to look out of a window and sketch the view. If you are lacking windows, then move to the hall or the playground.

◆ Move back to tables and colour in the sketches, using pastels or pencils of your choice; you could use paints instead.

◆ Ask children to make a window frame out of the sugar paper (this could be done in a numeracy lesson as a measuring activity!) and stick it over the scene they have created. Be careful not to cut through the frame, but to cut out the 'windows' from the inside first.

9. **Kings, queens and jacks**

You will need: A5 paper; pencils; felt-tipped pens; photocopier; playing cards; scissors; photocopier.

✦ Give each child a playing card depicting a king, queen or jack and get them to see that the picture is split in half with the same drawing rotated on the bottom half of the card.

✦ Give them each a piece of A5 paper that is portrait (short side up).

✦ Ask the children to draw a horizontal line across the page exactly halfway and ask the children to draw just the top-half picture. They may copy the playing card or base their ideas on it to create their own king, queen or jack.

✦ Colour the top half with felt-tipped pens and leave the bottom half blank.

✦ Photocopy their pictures and get the children to cut out the copy, rotate it and stick it on the bottom half, which they can leave black and white or colour.

✦ You can vary this idea with any picture, rotating it three times in a square split into quarters. This can be a useful link to pattern work in numeracy sessions, too.

10. Chocolate wrappers

You will need: empty chocolate-bar wrappers; pencils; felt-tipped pens or colouring pencils.

✦   Give each child a chocolate-bar wrapper and discuss what they can see. How many colours are used? What style of writing is depicted? Are there creases in the wrapper?

✦   Ask them to draw a chocolate-bar wrapper. You can either:

❖   Get them to design their own wrapper using first a pencil, then felt tips, making a flat design.

Or

❖   Copy the wrapper as an observational drawing, using coloured pencils and shading to make it look 3D.

✦   Make a display using their pictures, together with some of the real wrappers. A useful link to literacy work would be to create advertisements using persuasive writing!

11. Fizzy-drink cans

You will need: empty fizzy-drink cans; pencils; coloured pencils or pastels.

✦   Give each child, or pair of children, an empty fizzy-drink can.

✦   Ask them to draw the can, focusing on making it look round in shape by looking at the darks and lights in their shading.

✦   Another activity is to get the children to design a can of their own on a flat rectangular piece of card, then actually make it into a cylindrical can shape.

✦   The two ideas together will make a great wall display, especially combined with some of the children's own writing, ie slogans, advertisements and fictional recipes for drinks.

12. **Boxes (1)**

You will need: empty cereal boxes or similar; pencils; coloured pencils.

✦ Give each child an empty box and ask them to draw it to make it look 3D. Perhaps show them how first, as it is not always easy for children to obtain perspective (see illustration).

✦ They can leave the drawing as a black and white sketch or colour it with pencils. Alternatively, you can extend the artwork by photocopying their original sketches and grouping them together to create a more abstract piece, leaving some copies black and white and some coloured, or some larger than others.

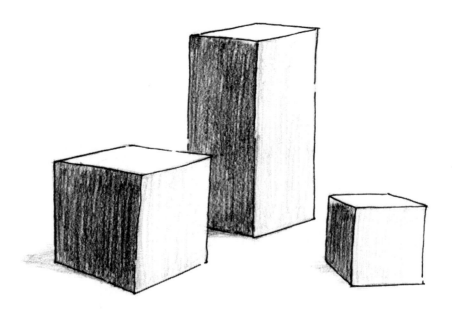

13. Boxes (2)

You will need: empty cardboard boxes (but not too large); A3 paper or thin cardboard; PVA glue; pencils; felt-tipped pens or other colouring media.

✦ Give each child a box and ask your group to carefully unfold the boxes so that they have a flat net in front of them.

✦ Discuss how the box is made to fold up into a 3D object.

✦ Get the children to draw around the flat boxes or create their own net, being careful not to forget to include tabs, which need to be glued later to hold the box together.

✦ Decorate the boxes, first using a sketching pencil to make sure nothing will appear upside down, then fold them up and stick them together.

✦ These look great displayed on a table or shelf in your classroom or stapled onto a wall!

14. **Nets – 3D extension**

You will need: thin card or paper (coloured); PVA glue; copies of nets (found in some numeracy support books or on the Internet).

✦ Let the children make other 3D shapes using formulated nets – or their own, if they are able. They could try making cylinders, triangular prisms, square or triangular-based pyramids.

✦ You can use different colours or designs of paper/card for your shapes, or when they are finished you could spray them in parts with silver or gold spray-paints (this should be done by an adult in a ventilated room – always follow instructions when using such art materials). Experiment with variations!

✦ Then, time permitting, you could suspend the 3D shapes using a needle and cotton from two crossed sticks to create collaborative mobiles to hang from the ceiling.

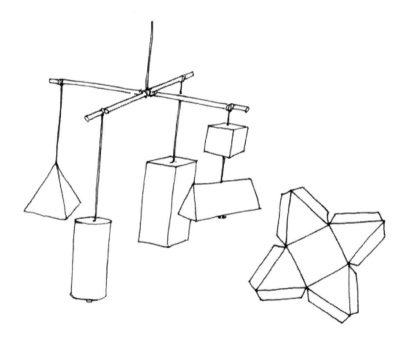

15. Spheres

You will need: coloured sugar paper; sketching pencils; charcoal; spherical objects.

✦ Look at some spherical objects together. Some ideas are: tennis ball, football, basketball, orange or an apple.

✦ Ask the children how they can make these objects appear round and not flat. Discuss where they can see light and shadow on the spheres.

✦ Ask the children to draw one of the objects, using shading to produce the effects they want. They can do these lightly with a sketching pencil, then go over them more neatly with their charcoal. Smudging the charcoal with their fingers will produce lighter shades of grey.

16. Symmetry patterns

You will need: A4 paper; 30cm rulers; fine pencils; felt-tipped pens.

✦ This is a simple way to produce a very complicated and impressive symmetrical pattern, and it is good for practising drawing skills using a ruler.

✦ Give the children a piece of A4 paper; they may choose which way up they turn it.

✦ Ask them to draw a straight line down the length of their paper. This line needs to be exactly in the middle, so they need to measure their distances.

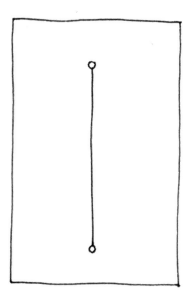

✦ Draw a dot near the top and bottom of this line, the same distance in from the bottom and top edges of the paper.

✦ Draw a dot anywhere to the left of the mid-line and measure the distance to draw another dot on the right side, so the dots are symmetrically placed.

✦   Draw straight lines from these dots to the dot at the top of the mid-line and to the dot at the bottom of the mid-line.

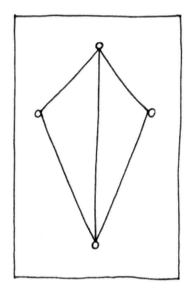

✦   Repeat this procedure, always drawing a dot on the left, then a dot on the right in its mirror image, then joining these dots to the top and bottom of the mid-line.

✦   A complex pattern will soon appear, which the children can then colour in with felt-tipped pens, also using symmetry with their chosen colours.

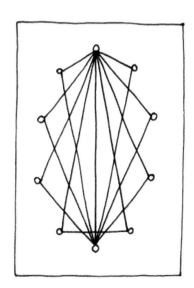

17. **Buildings in miniature**

You will need: previous sketches of buildings in the children's sketch books; white paper cut into small pieces (no larger than 7cm in length); fine pencils and one brown colouring pencil each.

✦ Remind the children of the sketches they did previously of buildings or parts of buildings.

✦ Explain that they are going to produce a miniature, showing them the paper you have cut.

✦ Ask them to draw a building, showing as much detail as possible. They must then shade all the paper, using shades of grey with their pencil and shades of brown with their colouring pencil. No other colours are to be used.

✦ You may vary this activity by using pen and inks, instead of pencils, or by using a portrait instead of a building as a focus for your miniature. Portraits look good drawn on oval paper, such as were popular when people carried miniature pictures of their loved ones inside lockets.

18. Jugs and mugs

You will need: sketching pencils; sugar paper; charcoal; white chalk.

✦   Show the children some jugs, mugs, cups or any other vessel that has an elliptical or oval at its top when seen from a certain angle.

✦   How can the children show this in their drawings? How can they show the roundness of the object?

✦   Look at where the handles are positioned, and look at where the light from the room is shining on the object.

✦   If you can, show the children some pictures by various artists of jugs and mugs and discuss how they have drawn/painted these objects.

✦   Ask the children to choose a jug or mug and draw it, going over it later with charcoal and white chalk to highlight the tones in the artwork.

19. Kitchen utensils

You will need: kitchen utensils (no knives!); sketching pencils; long pieces of paper of your choice.

◆　Show the children examples such as potato mashers, ice-cream scoops and ladles, preferably metal ones with wooden or plastic handles.

◆　Discuss the objects and what they are made from. Do the children notice any reflections in the metals? Does the light shine differently on the non-shiny materials? Can the children show the difference between wood, metal or plastic by adding shading or markings to their own drawings?

◆　Ask them to draw one of these objects trying to show the differences in texture of the materials the object is made from.

◆　You may use pencils, charcoals, colouring pencils or pastels for this activity.

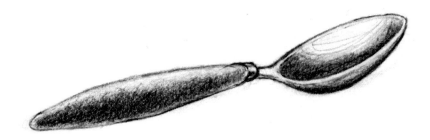

20. Half faces

You will need: pictures of a variety of faces cut out of magazines (preferably ones that will take up most of an A4 piece of paper); A4 paper; pencils.

✦ Cut your faces in half and stick one side of the face onto the sheet of A4 paper, leaving space for the children to draw the other side of the face.

✦ It is easier for left-handed children to draw on the left side of the paper and right-handed children to draw on the right.

✦ Get the children to look carefully at the one half of the face, then draw the other half on the sheet of paper.

✦ You can leave as a black and white sketch or add colour if you wish.

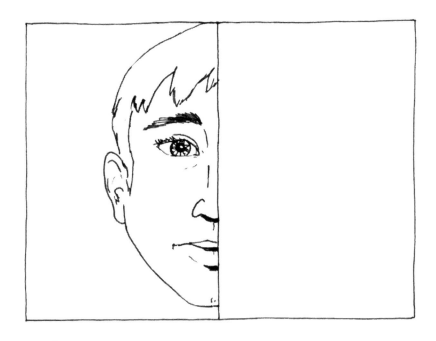

21. **Chinese landscapes**

You will need: pictures of landscapes from Chinese artists; sugar paper cut into long rectangles; charcoal; green, blue and pink chalks.

✦   Show the children the pictures and discuss where the prints originate from. How do they know this? How do the landscapes differ from British traditional landscapes? Which way up is the paper? Colours? Shades?

✦   Give each child a long rectangle of sugar paper, short side up. Ask them to sketch a landscape using their charcoal first and then add limited colours afterwards.

✦   Back on shiny red or gold paper and display with some of the prints from various Chinese artists.

22. **Straight line patterns**

You will need: pencils; paper; rulers.

✦ Give each child a piece of paper. First they must draw a line
10cm long horizontally mid-page. Mark each cm on the line.

✦ Then draw a vertical line 10cm long through the midpoint.
Again, mark each cm.

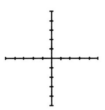

✦ Join the top mark to the first horizontal mark. Join the top
mark to the second horizontal mark and so on. Next join
the last mark on the horizontal line to the top mark on the
vertical, the second mark on the vertical, the third mark on
the vertical and so on.

✦ Rotate your pattern and repeat the above until each
remaining quarter of the pattern is complete.

✦ Children may choose coloured pencils, if they are able to do
this without mistakes, and experiment with different colour
schemes.

23. **Drawing people using ovals**

You will need: pencils; paper; coloured pencils or pens of your choice.

✦ On a board, show the children how to draw a figure using ovals. Each part of the body will be a different oval. To draw the leg, for example, use one oval for the foot, one for the calf

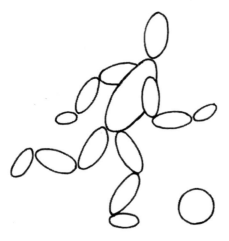

✦ Begin with the head, then form the body, adding limb shapes to create a moving body, eg a footballer or a ballerina.

✦ Sketch the ovals lightly at first, then go over them to add in features or clothing.

24. Grid enlargements

You will need: grid photocopied onto plastic photocopiable sheets (see page 122); paper; pictures; pencils; colours of your choice.

✦ Give each child an A5-size plastic sheet with a grid made up of nine rectangular segments (photocopy grid on page 122 onto clear plastic sheets).

✦ Ask them to lay it over part of a picture from a book or magazine. You may choose pictures of one theme. For example, you could choose the work of one artist, parts of animals or people or buildings.

✦ Next give them an A4 or A3 sheet of paper that is split into nine rectangular segments exactly like the plastic photocopy.

✦ They must then copy each section from the original picture onto their own paper, making an enlargement of that section.

✦ Display some of the work next to the original pictures.

25. Totem poles

You will need: sugar paper; pencils; thin charcoals; oil pastels; pictures of Native American totem poles; totem pole template (see page 123).

✦ Look at the pictures of the totem poles and discuss why the Native Americans make them.

✦ Ask the children to draw their own designs of totem poles. Colour using pastels and charcoal outlines. Felt-tipped pens are another option.

✦ As a follow-on from this activity, you could ask the children to make a collaborative totem pole using cardboard boxes. Each pair or group of children could decorate one cardboard box with a mixed media of your choice. The boxes can be stuck on top of each other to create a large 3D totem pole for a hall (use thin card covered in tissue paper to make top wings, as you will need them to be light).

✦ Clay can also be used for a totem pole. Roll the clay out like pastry to about 1cm thick – no thinner, or it will be too fragile. Children can then use the stencil on page 123 to get a basic shape. You then have a clay totem pole to be patterned using various clay tools, or painted, or both. Don't try to lift the totem poles until they are completely flat.

26. Design a banknote

You will need: foreign banknotes or pictures of notes; pencils; felt-tipped pens.

✦ Look at all the various banknotes and discuss the details, patterns and information that is included.

✦ Ask the children to design and make their own banknotes for a fictional country.

27. Design a chair

You will need: pencils; paper; pictures of chairs.

✦ Find lots of pictures of chairs, and find examples of both old and modern designs.

✦ Discuss these with the children. Are they old/new? In which room would they be used? Are they garden chairs? Are they for old or young people? What are the chairs made from? Are they ornate? Plain?

✦ Get your children to design a chair for a specific room/age range.

✦ Link this to some literacy work. For instance, the children could write about their design, saying what materials would be used, who the chair is for and where in a house or garden the chair would be placed.

28. **Design a garden**

You will need: paper; pencils and coloured pencils.

◆ Look at some garden designs by professional landscape gardeners. If you know a person who could visit the school to discuss their profession, this would be very useful.

◆ Discuss how the plans are laid out, ie the plan is seen from above, not drawn in 3D.

◆ Tell the children they are going to design a small garden especially for young children. This garden needs to appeal to the infants' senses, namely sight, smell, sound and touch. Also, the garden needs to be safe and not include any toxic plants or hard, sharp edges.

◆ Brainstorm ideas – perhaps no pond or steps in view of safety. Herbs or fragrant flowers could be included for smell, wind chimes for sound, bright colours or a sculpture for sight and foliage for touch.

◆ Show the designs to the head teacher; perhaps he/she could be persuaded to get one of the designs made into a real garden.

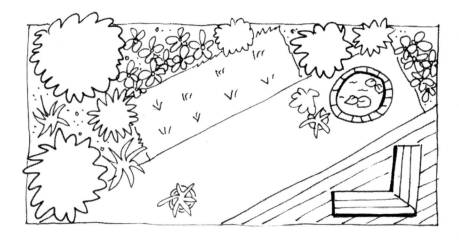

29. Design a board game

You will need: pencils; paper; coloured pencils.

✦ Look at some familiar simple board games, for example snakes and ladders.

✦ How does the game work? Who is it for? What makes it fun? What makes it work?

✦ Get the children to design their own board game for a specific age range. They could work in pairs for this activity. Maybe they could base their game on a theme such as a space mission, rainforest adventure or sea voyage.

✦ Make a rough copy. Play the game to see if it works. Make any improvements to the game or alterations. Discuss which colours could be used for the board/counters.

✦ If you have time, follow up this activity in another session by asking children to make the games themselves on thick cardboard bases. They can then play each other's games and see which ones work the best.

30. Design an outfit

You will need: pencils; paper; coloured pencils.

✦   Look at some designs drawn by fashion designers. You could find these on the Internet, or find a real designer who may send you some colour photocopies of their own work.

✦   Discuss these with the children, and then give them the task of designing an outfit themselves.

✦   They need to think what purpose the outfit is for. It could be for a smart occasion, casual dress or seasonal summer or winter wear. They will also need to think about who the outfit is being designed for. Is it a man, woman, child or baby?

✦   Draw some rough designs on paper first and experiment with colour. Think about accessories such as belts, bags, scarves and shoes to add to the design.

✦   Put the final designs together and display.

31. Shade cards

You will need: liquid paints; palettes or plastic pots; shade cards from DIY shops; brushes; thin card.

✦ Show the children the shade cards you have collected from the paint departments of your local DIY shops.

✦ Tell the children they are going to make their own shade cards.

✦ They must choose one colour and white – do not use black. First, paint a neat white strip across your card; then add a minute portion of colour to the white. Just covering a few bristles is enough. Paint another strip across. Add a tiny bit more of coloured paint to the white.

✦ The children may not see much difference at first, as this will be a gradual change of colour, but as they progress and the paints dry, they will see shades appearing. They need to avoid adding too much colour or they will not end up with this gradation.

Display all shade cards in your classroom!

32. Distorted faces

You will need: pictures of distorted faces by various artists (Picasso was particularly good at these!); paints; brushes; pencils.

✦ Show the children the pictures of distorted faces to get across the idea of doing something in an abstract way.

✦ Get the children to draw an abstract face with all its features in different places.

✦ Ask the children to paint their sketched faces but using only shades of blue or shades of red. Give them only one colour and white paint so they must mix all the shades themselves.

✦ Display the faces with blues together and reds together. Do the blue faces look cold or sad? Do the red faces appear warmer and more cheerful? Did they enjoy the idea of doing abstract? Discuss.

33. Black, white and shades of grey

You will need: paper; black and white paints; thin brushes; pencils; pens; pastels and chalks in only black, white and grey or silver.

✦ Ask the children to draw a wiggly line over their paper, creating segments to fill in.

✦ Paint each section of the pattern in white, black or shades of grey.

✦ Once the patterns are completely dry, go over each section with pastels or pens, making intricate patterns in contrasting shades, so dark 'topping' patterns go on light-painted parts and vice versa. Silver or metallic grey also add a great effect if you have them.

34. **Concentric circles**

You will need: pictures by artists who have used circles to create patterns (eg Bridget Riley); pairs of compasses; pencils; paper; paints; thin brushes.

✦ Show the children some examples of artists' work depicting patterns using circles. Discuss.

✦ Ask the children to draw circles within circles using their pairs of compasses. They may also use part circles to fill the space or overlapping circles (see picture below). Draw a simple example on a board to show the class.

✦ Ask them to choose only two of the three primary colours (blue, red and yellow). They may mix any colours using the two chosen.

✦ Carefully paint the circular patterns with the thin brushes. Leave one area to dry before painting an area next to it!

35. **Townscapes**

You will need: blue and red paint; brushes; A3 paper; black sugar paper; gold paper.

✦   Explain to the children that they are going to create a background using various purples. They will be given only blue and red paints, and so will have to mix their own colours. The purples will give the effect of a night sky.

✦   They can create their own sky using stripes or swirling patterns. It is up to them to experiment, but you want to see lots of different purples!

✦   Once the backgrounds are drying, the children can then cut out silhouettes of buildings using the black sugar paper. They could make skyscrapers for a city scene or a religious building and houses for a townscape.

✦   Use the gold paper to show lights through windows, the moon or any other lights such as street lamps.

✦   This idea can be used with red and yellow paints to create a sunset scene. Perhaps the children could cut out a silhouette of a tropical island or a palm tree to stick onto it.

36. **Camouflage animals**

You will need: pictures of animals; A3 paper; various paints; brushes; scissors.

✦ Talk about animals that use their colourings to camouflage themselves. Make a list: cheetah, leopard, lizard, moth, tropical fish, zebra, polar bear. Discuss why animals do this and look at some of the pictures you have found.

✦ The children need to choose an animal and find a picture of it from magazines or the Internet. Make sure the picture is about A4 size. They may find just the head of an animal, which is fine, if it is fairly big.

✦ Using paints, they must create a background that will camouflage the animal; for example a yellow and black-spotted background can be painted for a cheetah, black and white curvy stripes for a zebra, brown shades or a bark pattern to hide a moth. The backgrounds can be realistic or abstract.

✦ Once the backgrounds are dry, put the animal picture onto card and place a square of thicker card onto the back of it. This will make the animal physically stand out on the paper, although your eyes will see it as blended into the background.

37. **Planet scenes**

You will need: A3 black sugar paper; various paints and different-size brushes; cardboard circle stencils or pairs of compasses; pictures of the solar system.

✦ This is a great link to learning about the solar system in science. Show the children a poster or pictures of our solar system.

✦ Look at the planets and how they differ in size or colour. Do they have rings like Saturn or moons like Earth? How is the Sun depicted? Talk about how an artist could show the Sun, which is made from gases, as opposed to a planet that is made from rock. Are the planets shown in 2D or 3D? Discuss what the children like about the planets, and how they move around the Sun.

✦ Explain to the children that they are going to create their own solar system, making up planets in any way they like. They can add stars or meteorites as they see fit. They can make it look 2D or 3D.

✦ Give them pencils and circle stencils or pairs of compasses so they can plan their scene lightly on the black sugar paper.

✦ Let them paint their planet scenes and display when dry.

(Top Tip – Flicking the bristles of the paintbrush near the paper gives a great starry effect, but be careful as the paint can travel if children get over-enthusiastic!)

38. Tessellating shapes

You will need: cardboard; wax crayons; watercolours (or watered-down paint); brushes; backing paper.

✦ This activity links well to maths. Talk first about the concept of tessellating shapes, and show the children some examples that could be utilized: equilateral triangles, squares, rectangles, hexagons, some jigsaw pieces and irregular shapes. Examples of these can be found in maths resource books or on the Internet.

✦ Ask each table of children to work as a group, first choosing one shape that will tessellate. They will need to make one stencil (approx A4 size) of that shape out of cardboard that they can then share to draw round.

✦ Ask each member of the group to cut out one of these shapes from the remaining cardboard.

✦ When they each have got a cardboard shape, they must decorate it with intricate patterns of their choice using wax crayons. Leave some space free of wax, because once the shape is decorated sufficiently, each child is going to go to the painting table and paint over the cardboard shape using different colours of paint. The wax will resist the paint and the watercolours should run into each other, leaving a painted pattern with the wax pattern still remaining.

✦ The child can leave this to dry and do a second shape using the group stencil if there is time.

✦ When the shapes are dry, the children must work together again as a team and stick all their shapes onto big sheets of backing paper, creating one big tessellating pattern. These look very effective put up on classroom walls or in school corridors!

39. **Contrasting colour wheel**

You will need: thin card; pencils; pairs of compasses; protractors; red, yellow and blue paints; thin brushes.

✦   There are variations on the idea of contrasting colour wheels, but the common concept is that some colours contrast better with others and therefore may be used so that one colour can offset the other to stand out more. Making a contrasting colour wheel that you can keep as a reference is useful for future activities with all media, not just paint.

✦   First, draw a circle using a pair of compasses. Then split the circle into six equal parts. This is a great link to mathematical work, comprising fractions, shape and accurate measuring of angles with a protractor.

✦   Paint one section red, leave a section, paint the next one blue, leave a section and then paint the next one yellow.

✦   Mix the red and blue paint to make purple and paint the section in between red and blue on the colour wheel purple.

✦   Mix yellow and red to make orange and fill in the section between red and yellow.

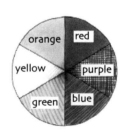

✦   Finally, mix blue and yellow to produce green to fill the section in between blue and yellow.

✦   When the circles are finished and dry, cut them out and then take a look at them together.

✦   Which colour is directly opposite to blue on the colour wheel? Orange. Blue and orange are therefore contrasting colours. Likewise, red is opposite to green, and yellow is opposite to purple. Keep these colour wheels somewhere easily accessible, perhaps stuck into a sketchbook, and have them ready for the next activity.

40. **Using contrasting colours**

You will need: paper or card cut into squares (28cm x 28cm); rulers; pencils; shape stencils; red, yellow and blue paint; thin brushes; mixing palettes.

✦ First, divide your square into four equal parts using a ruler and pencil line.

✦ Choose a stencil shape that will fit the resulting squares, eg a hexagon, and draw a hexagon in each quarter. The shape does not have to be central and can be placed differently in each part.

✦ Look at your colour wheel from the previous activity and choose two contrasting colours, eg blue and orange. You will then use only blues and oranges, no other colour.

✦ Paint your first hexagon in any design using the oranges, and the background of the first quarter in different blues.

✦ The next hexagon can be reversed so you have an orange background, but with blues in the hexagon and so on.

✦ Continue in the same way, experimenting with your contrasting colours until the entire big square is complete.

✦ Back your work on orange paper then double-back it onto blue paper, which adds to the effect of contrasting colours. Display on a wall and enjoy!

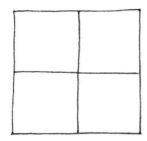 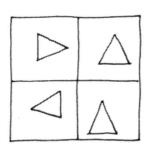 

Painting ideas

41. **Pebbles and shells**

You will need: paper or sketching books; sketching pencils; paints; thin brushes; pale grey sugar paper; pictures of pebbles (both photographic and work by artists).

✦   If you are lucky enough to live by the sea, get some extra adults and take your children to the beach with their sketchbooks and make some observational drawings of pebbles.

✦   If you live inland, ask the children to bring in any pebbles they may have and do the same thing in your classroom. Failing that, sketch from photographic pictures (the Internet is a great source for this).

✦   Look at the patterns, shades, markings, colours and texture of the pebbles.

✦   Next, look at some pictures or photographs of pebbles made by various artists. How have the artists arranged the pebbles? Have they used lots or just three, for example? How have they made the pebbles look 3D instead of 2D? Discuss.

✦   Ask your children to sketch a pebble on the grey sugar paper and then to paint it in detail, using shades to get the 3D effect. If they have time they may choose to paint more than one, but quality, not quantity, is the aim here.

✦   Once dry, cut out the pebbles and arrange them in the style of one of your favourite artists that you have discussed previously.

✦   The same activity can be done using shells instead of pebbles. Remind children to return anything they have borrowed to the beach!

42. **Making waves**

You will need: pictures of waves (both photographic and work by artists); paper; blue and white paint; thin brushes.

✦ Look at your pictures of waves. Discuss the difference between photographic pictures and those created by artists. An interesting print is 'The Great Wave' created by Japanese artist Katsushika Hokusai.

✦ Ask your children to create a wave scene. They will be allowed to use only blue and white paint, so remind them about mixing the paint to obtain a multitude of shades. Leave the choice open as to whether they paint a realistic scene, or try out an idea based on the work of one of the artists already discussed.

43. **Bridges**

You will need: pictures of bridges; thick paper (or thin card); pencils; watercolours; black, brown and red pencils; chalks and pastels (optional).

✦ Look at your bridge pictures and discuss. Are the bridges old or new? Which materials were used to make them? How were they made? Why are some bridges like Sydney Harbour Bridge and Tower Bridge famous, and others not? Are they ornate? Why were they made – to cross a river, the sea, a lake, a mountain pass or a railway track?

✦ Discuss the backgrounds. If the bridge goes over water, does it have a reflection?

✦ The children are to paint a background using watercolours. If they have not used these before, give them a rough piece of paper so that they can try them out first. The idea is that the children brush the water on first, then add small amounts of colour and blend the colours into the water. Colours will run into each other, so make sure one section is dry if you wish to prevent this.

✦ Once the background is dry, draw your bridge, first using a sketching pencil lightly.

✦ Go over the sketch, using a coloured pencil. This could be black for iron, brown for wood or even red for metal. Put in as much detail as you can. You could add in small brickwork or ornate designs.

✦ If the bridge crosses water and needs a reflection, add this in too, using a media of your choice (for example chalks, pastels, and coloured pencils).

✦ Display the best creations with some of the pictures or photographs you used earlier in the activity.

44. **Historical portraits**

You will need: pictures of historical figures; A3 paper; paints; thin brushes; sketching pencils.

✦ This is a lovely link to history. Look at various portraits from the period in question. You could use a Tudor, a Victorian or an ancient Egyptian.

✦ Discuss the idea of a portrait. Look at the features shown; eyes are actually in the middle of the head rather than at the top. Discuss the clothing, head attire or jewellery. Is the person rich or poor? Are they cheerful, sad or serious?

✦ Ask the children to sketch a rough portrait of a person from the historical period chosen. They are only to draw a face, neck and the tops of the shoulders, using as much of the paper's length as they can. Do not draw the whole body.

✦ This could be someone famous, such as a king, queen or politician, or a fictional character, perhaps a poor beggar or rich Victorian lady. They need to use the paper to fit the subject, with the longer lengths at the side. You could also choose to use large ovals as a variation to a rectangle.

✦ Use thin brushes to paint the portrait. Remember to take a lot of time on these, especially if your figure has an elaborate period costume. Back onto black sugar paper and display.

45. **Historical or religious buildings**

You will need: pictures of buildings; paints; brushes; paper; sketching pencils.

✦ Buildings often come up when you're studying a particular topic in history or religious education, so why not have a go at painting some of them?

✦ Get the children to look closely at pictures of the building they wish to base their ideas on. Examples include the Pyramids in Egypt, the Acropolis in Greece, Westminster Abbey in England, a medieval castle, a bomb-damaged terraced house during World War Two, a mosque or a Buddhist temple.

✦ Try adding things to your paint to enhance effects. If you are painting an Egyptian pyramid, add some sand and PVA glue to the paint, or if you are painting a mosque, you could add gold glitter to make the ornate domes more elaborate. PVA glue or flour will thicken paint and give it texture when it dries. Experiment and have fun!

✦ An alternative activity is to make buildings 3D, using boxes, tubes and cardboard etc. Use masking tape to join these together, as paint will not cover transparent sticky tape, and cover any plastic-coated card with paper, so when you add paint later it will cover more easily. This is a good group activity and the buildings look great on a fabric-covered table.

46. **Descriptive paintwork**

You will need: a descriptive text (or use the text provided); red, yellow and blue paints; thin brushes; A3 paper.

✦   This is a wonderful link to literacy and an activity that really stretches the imagination!

✦   Choose a suitable short text from a book, either prose or poetry, or use the one I have written below. It needs to be a text full of descriptive language. It could be a description of a landscape, person, mythical creature or scene.

✦   Read it twice to the children, a third time if necessary. They must then paint the picture that they have conjured up in their minds whilst listening to the readings of the text.

✦   Later on, you may wish to read the text again so that the children can add in any details they may have missed. Alternatively, put a copy of the text on an overhead projector or computer screen for reference.

Firebird by Paula Goodridge

" … then I woke up in the most amazing place. I was in a beautiful, tropical garden, surrounded by leafy plants, and flowers of all colours, shapes and sizes, all of which I had never seen in my life before. A colourful parrot-like bird was perched on a tree close by, its long red and orange feathers drooping downwards, curling at the ends like bright flames. The garden was closed off by a stone wall covered in creepers, some tall hedges and a few large trees dotted with blossoms, but in the distance, through the trees, I could just see an old castle on a hilltop. Nothing else was near it. It stood alone. No people were there. I was alone in this fantasy garden, just the firebird and me. I felt warm with the sun shining and I felt peaceful, but why was I there?"

---

47. **Glass jars**

You will need: glass jars; glass paints (available from art shops and suppliers); thin brushes; tea-light candles.

✦ This makes a nice little gift for a family member or friend!

✦ Give each child a small glass jar. Remind them of safety when handling glass.

✦ Ask them to decorate their jars with intricate patterns using the glass paints.

✦ Once dry, put a tea-light candle inside each jar and give them to parents/friends. Younger children may need to transport this home in a cardboard box to avoid accidents!

48. **Watercolour landscapes**

You will need: pictures of landscapes; watercolours; brushes; watercolour paper.

✦ Look at some pictures of landscapes or, if possible, go out for a walk in the countryside and do some sketches of landscapes.

✦ Ask the children to very lightly draw a rough outline of a landscape on their paper.

✦ Carefully, paint the scenes using watercolours. If you have not used them before with your children, it is worth having a practice-go on a piece of scrap paper beforehand. The best method is to spread the water on first, then blend in a small amount of paint and move the colour around. Make sure one section is dry before painting an area next to it, or the colours will run.

49. # Thick-paint landscapes

You will need: PVA glue or flour; red, blue and yellow paints; brushes; cardboard; pictures of landscapes (which can be cut up).

✦ Stick part of a landscape picture onto the cardboard. This can be any shape. The children are going to paint in the rest of the scene.

✦ To make it more of a challenge, give them only red, yellow and blue paint so they have to mix colours. Also, add flour or PVA glue to the paints so that they will thicken up. The children can experiment with how much they add in. Once dried, the paints leave fabulous textures.

50. # Household objects

You will need: pencils, A3 paper; black and white paints; thin brushes; household objects (eg, a mug, cup and saucer, a potato masher, a ladle and a wooden ornament).

✦ Show the children some of the objects and discuss the shapes, materials and tones seen in each object.

✦ Ask them to sketch one object so that it looks 3D. This is achieved with shading.

✦ Next, give the children black and white paint and get them to paint the object, using darks and lights in shades of grey to give the painting form. The entire object needs to be painted.

✦ Once dry, add in a coloured background using chalks, pastels or pale watercolours.

✦ Display the paintings together with some of the household objects.

51. **Paint to music**

You will need: two tracks of music of your choice – one very slow, soft and calming and the other fast, powerful and uplifting ; A3 paper; paints; brushes.

✦ Give each child a piece of paper and ask them to draw a line diagonally from one corner to the other.

✦ Play them the first piece of music and get them to close their eyes and listen to it.

✦ Play this again several times and ask them to paint the first triangle on the sheet. They must paint whatever comes into their minds when listening to the music. Does it make them think of a particular colour? Object? Feeling? How can they show this on paper? The painting can be realistic or abstract. They can paint patterns as well as things, if that is what they wish to do.

✦ Repeat this activity with the second, faster piece of music and then get children to fill in the second triangle on their sheet.

✦ At the end of the session, sit down and get volunteers to explain the thinking behind their creations.

Aboriginal-style Art

Aboriginal art represents and symbolizes the world and beliefs of its people. Historically, the people used the resources around them, creating rock art, body painting or ground mosaics, for example. Children love creating their own works in the Aboriginal style; the activities below have all been tried and tested with great success, either individually or as a mini-topic. First, do some research of your own, either from books or the Internet, so that you can give the children some background in the culture and art of the Aboriginal people. Try to collect lots of pictures of art by Aboriginal artists so that you can use them as a stimulus for your children. Discuss these before you start an activity.

52. Aboriginal-style animals

You will need: paints in red, yellow, orange, brown and white; animal shapes cut out of black sugar paper; cotton-wool buds or old pencils.

✦ This is a good activity for younger or less able children. Give them each a native Australian animal shape cut from black sugar paper. You could use a turtle, snake, kangaroo or a fish.

✦ Show them how to decorate their animal by creating patterns using dots only. Cotton-wool buds or the end of an old pencil create more circular dots than a paintbrush. Try to encourage them to make patterns like spirals or concentric circles, rather than putting dots randomly.

53. Aboriginal-style plan views

You will need: paints in red, yellow, orange, brown and white; cotton-wool buds or old pencils; A3 black or brown sugar paper.

✦ Many Aboriginal artists created 'plan view' art, whereby the art represented perhaps a camp near a stream or hunting ground. Find some of these pictures from a book or the Internet to show the children.

✦ Get them to create their own 'plan view' using this method. They must use only dots to do this.

54. **Didgeridoos**

You will need: cardboard tubes; paints and pencils in red, yellow, orange and white; and black or brown paint.

✦ Show the children a real didgeridoo if you can get one, or, failing that, pictures of various decorated didgeridoos. Discuss these with your children.

✦ Give each child, or pair of children, a cardboard tube and get them to paint the entire thing black or brown. Leave these to dry.

✦ Ask the children to decorate their didgeridoos, using dots to create typical Aboriginal patterns.

55. **Balsa boomerangs**

You will need: boomerang shapes cut from balsa wood; paints; pencils.

✦ Show the children real boomerangs if you can, and discuss why and how they were used (boomerangs were used as a hunting tool, not as a plaything).

✦ Give children a balsa-wood boomerang and get them to decorate it in the Aboriginal style.

Display all your artwork, artefacts and pictures to make a really impressive gallery!

56. Tie-dyeing (knot-dyeing)

You will need: white or pale cream cotton fabric (lining fabric for curtains is good) approximately the size of A3 paper; cold dye; dye fixer; plastic buckets; drying rack or newspaper on a table; plastic gloves.

✦ Follow the instructions on the dye and fixer packets to make up your buckets beforehand. If you have not dyed before, you may wish to begin with using just one colour.

✦ You can use dyes that require warm water and salt instead of fixer, but cold dyes are generally safer when working with young children.

✦ Give each child a piece of fabric and get them to tie as many knots in it as they can. The knots can overlap, but need to be pulled tight.

✦ One by one the children may then, wearing plastic gloves, put the knotted fabric into the fixer and into the dye.

✦ Leave for as long as the instructions on the packet indicate. Take the knotted material out, lay on the drying rack and remember to place a label with the child's name next to it.

✦ Once the material has mostly dried to a slightly damp feel, ask the children to undo their knots. The material will have a lovely pattern on it.

✦ Hang up the pieces of fabric to dry completely.

✦ If you fancy using two colours, put more knots in after this and repeat the activity using another colour.

57. **String dyeing**

You will need: white or pale cream cotton fabric (lining fabric for curtains is good) approximately the size of A3 paper; cold dye; dye fixer; plastic buckets; drying rack or newspaper on a table; plastic gloves; string.

✦ Follow the instructions as given in Tie-dyeing (activity 56), but instead of putting knots into the fabric, scrunch it up and tie string around the scrunched part. The string must be very tight and securely tied or the pattern will not work.

✦ Undo or cut the string when the material is dry. You should be left with a tie-dyed circle when the material is unfolded.

✦ Again, you can use another colour, repeating the activity with more tied string. Keep the string tight!

✦ You can do this on white T-shirts if your budget can run to it. The children will love to wear something they have dyed.

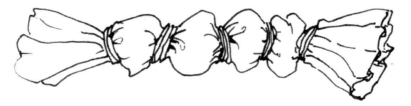

58. **Elastic-band dyeing in half-and-half colours**

You will need: white or pale cream cotton fabric (lining fabric for curtains is good) approximately the size of A3 paper; cold dye in 2 colours; dye fixer; plastic buckets; drying rack or newspaper on a table; plastic gloves; elastic bands.

✦ You can experiment with tying elastic bands around your pieces of fabric before you dye them for another effect. Again, make sure the bands are very tight.

✦ If you dip one half of the fabric in one colour then the other half in another colour, you again have yet another effect using the simple dyeing method from the first activity.

59. **Fan-shape dyeing**

You will need: white or pale cream cotton fabric (lining fabric for curtains is good) approximately the size of A3 paper; cold dye; dye fixer; plastic buckets; drying rack or newspaper on a table; plastic gloves; string

✦ We have all made a paper fan on a hot day by folding a piece of paper accordion-style. If you do this with fabric, securing it at the ends with an elastic band, you have yet another effect when the material is dyed!

60. **Collaborative dyeing**

You will need: an old white sheet; washing-machine dye.

✦ Get each child to choose one of the dyeing methods introduced so far (eg tie-dyeing or string-dyeing), and let them all prepare a section of the old sheet.

✦ Take it home and put it in your washing machine, following the instructions on the dye packet.

✦ Bring the dyed sheet back into school when it is dry and show your group of children. They will be astonished at the patterns and really pleased to see something big displayed in their room as a wall hanging or a table cover for a display!

61. **Fabric square in shades**

You will need: mixed fabrics of varying colours cut up into small pieces; felt squares (approximately 15cm x 15cm); buttons; sequins; threads, ribbons; PVA glue or needles and thread; scissors.

✦ The children are going to choose one felt square each. The colour they choose will be the colour they work with throughout the activity.

✦ If the child has chosen purple, his/her next task is to find as many materials (eg ribbons and threads) as possible in shades of purple.

✦ Next, the children will use all these bits and pieces to make a collage on their felt square. Materials may overlap, or be placed on top of each other, but completely at random. This is not supposed to look like anything but abstract, which children sometimes find hard to grasp. Try to prevent them this time from trying to make a 'real picture'.

✦ Sequins and buttons can be put on at the end.

✦ Whether the children glue the bits on or sew them is up to you. Sewing takes longer but lifts the quality, but it depends on your children's experience and ability with the use of a needle. You could let them use glue for some fabrics and a needle and thread to sew on others.

✦ Encourage them to make the collages as detailed as possible.

✦ Display your squares individually, or sew them all together to make a big, eye-catching wall hanging!

62. Contrasting colours in fabrics

You will need: red, blue, yellow, green, orange and purple felts; PVA glue; needles and thread; scissors.

✦ Revise the concept of contrasting colours (see activity 39).

✦ Ask the children to choose two contrasting colours, eg red and green.

✦ Choose a background felt square in one of the colours, eg red.

✦ Cut out lots of triangles of various sizes in the other colour (green, in this case) and stick or sew them onto the background.

✦ Find sequins, buttons or ribbons in the same colour as the background, and add them on top of the green.

✦ Display your fabulous patterns!

63. **Christmas stockings**

You will need: pencils; felt; stocking stencil; PVA glue or needles and thread; sequins; ribbons and buttons.

✦ Give each child a simple stocking stencil and ask them to cut out two stocking shapes in felt of their choice.

✦ Cut a piece of ribbon to make a loop. This will attach the stocking to your tree!

✦ Glue or sew the felt pieces together, inserting the ribbon loop, so that it is firmly attached.

✦ You could decorate your stockings with sequins, ribbons or buttons.

64. **Glove puppets**

You will need: felt; glove puppet stencil (see page 124); glue or needles and threads; wool; buttons; scraps of fabrics.

✦ Prepare a stencil of your hand to make a glove puppet. (You could use the stencil on page 124, enlarged if necessary.)

✦ Use the stencil to cut two glove puppet shapes from felt.

✦ Stick or sew these together, leaving the bottom open for your hand.

✦ Decorate each puppet as you wish, using wool for hair and buttons for eyes.

✦ Children will love making up scripts for a puppet play afterwards, so this is a great link to play writing in literacy. They could perform to the infants!

65. **Batik fish**

You will need: batik resist; pieces of fabric; fabric dyes; examples/photographs of batik.

✦ A liquid resist material is now available from art supplies companies, and avoids the use of hot wax (once the common way of producing batik). It can be used cold and painted onto material quite easily.

✦ Batik is thought to have developed in Asia and spread from there; it is now practised all over the world. The idea is that a picture or pattern is designed in batik liquid/wax on the material, and then the material is dyed, leaving the pattern/picture free of dye, because the batik liquid/wax resists the dye.

✦ First the children need to look at some examples/photographs of batik and to discuss the origins and concepts of the batik method.

✦ Next, they need to plan a design. Fish are relatively simple to design, but you could design patterns, faces, flowers etc. Once the child has a good rough design on paper, they will need to paint their design onto a piece of fabric using the batik resist liquid. Always follow the manufacturer's guidelines.

✦ Finally, put the material into a dye bath (see activity 56 for more information), then remove and leave to dry.

✦ One colour is generally sufficient for beginners, but if you wish to use another colour, simply add more batik resist material to the original picture and dye the material again.

✦ The batik method could be used on a T-shirt or, if pupils work collaboratively, on a big sheet of material. Remember to put card or newspaper inside the T-shirt so that the resist material does not go through to the back.

66. **Batik printing patterns**

You will need: batik resist; pieces of fabric; fabric dyes; stamps or sponges for printing; shallow dish.

✦ Instead of using a brush to paint a picture onto the fabric (as in activity 65), the children could use stamps or sponges to combine printing with textiles. Put the resist material into a shallow dish and dip the printing tools into it. Print onto the fabric, and then dye the material.

✦ Patterns are ideal for beginners. Children could experiment with repeated geometric, mosaic or abstract patterns depending on your/their choice.

✦ Using another colour and repeating this method would further the challenge, so you could include the use of contrasting colours or shades again.

Art Activities

67. **Simple bookmarks**

You will need: binca canvas; embroidery threads and needles; scissors.

✦ Binca canvas can be bought on-line or from various art supplies stores. There is also a plastic version which younger children or children with special needs sometimes find easier to use. Either type is great for this activity.

✦ Cut a rectangle out of the canvas, approximately 8cm x 20cm, and give one to each child.

✦ Show the children how to thread their needles, then demonstrate a simple running stitch going lengthways up or down the canvas. There is no need to knot or finish off with this; the children may leave about 2cm length of thread at either end. This you can neaten up at the end with scissors.

✦ Children can choose their own colour schemes, for example random, contrasting or repeated colours. Start a new coloured piece of thread for each line.

✦ When finished, neaten up the ends with a pair of scissors and use your bookmark in your favourite book!

✦ Once the children are able to use needle and thread sufficiently, you may choose to create samplers, and use a different type of stitch for each line on a piece of binca canvas, leaving spaces in between. You could also teach the children how to do cross-stitch so that they can create their own patterns using just this one stitch on a smallish square of binca canvas. Large pieces can take a lot of time!

68. **Peg-loom weaving**

You will need: peg looms; wool; string.

✦ Peg looms can be bought on-line or from various art stores. If your budget allows, buy a fairly small peg loom for each child. Alternatively, this could also be done as group work.

✦ A peg loom is a rectangular block of wood or plastic with holes in one side into which the pegs fit. Each peg has holes in it and you need to string these up before you begin. Follow manufacturers' instructions or look up weaving websites for more help. Initially this sounds complicated, but once you have done one, it becomes very simple.

✦ Once you have strung your loom, the children then take pieces of wool and weave in and out of the pegs.

✦ When they reach the top of the pegs, pull the peg out of its hole, push the weaving down the string and then insert the empty peg back in its hole. Do this with each peg, and then the child can carry on weaving until he/she reaches the top of the pegs and the whole thing is repeated over and over.

✦ The weaving will travel down the strings. Once the strings are full, they will feel tight. Cut the strings, again, follow the instructions given with each peg loom, and the children have a piece of woollen weaving which they could stick onto a card or hang up on a wall.

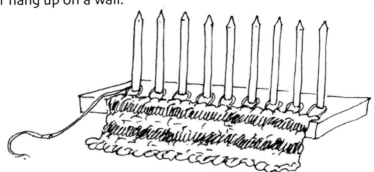

Art Activities

69. Rag rugs

You will need: larger peg looms (size dependent on the size of rug you want); thin strips of fabric; string.

✦ The method for this activity is exactly the same as the previous one. The difference is that you use a bigger peg loom and that, instead of wool, you are using long strips (eg 1m) of fabric. This is a good way to recycle fabrics. Any will do as long as they are clean. You may also use ribbons, if anyone has any spare to donate. Children can knot each strip together or simply overlap the strips for a smoother rug.

✦ Once the weaving is complete, it may be used as a rug or a wall hanging. Add a special touch by sewing a few strips to the bottom, with sequins or beads attached.

70. **William Morris inspired**

You will need: textiles; artefacts or pictures showing designs by William Morris; some background history of his life; card, pencils; coloured pencils; pieces of plain white or cream fabric; fabric pens.

◆ KS2 love a challenge, so before this activity ask them to find out some information about the designer William Morris (1834–1896). They can do this in their spare time or at home. The Internet has a wealth of information. Encourage them to make notes in their sketchbooks or stick in any pictures they like showing his designs.

◆ Familiarize yourself too with his works. The William Morris Gallery in London has a website and provides information for teachers. Collect any artefacts or prints with his designs, especially any textiles. Some scarves, curtains and bed linen today have designs on them that have been inspired by Morris.

◆ Gather together all your artefacts and evaluate your findings with the children.
   ❖ Who was Morris?
   ❖ What did he do?
   ❖ What is an interior designer?
   ❖ Do the children know any interior designers from television today (for example Laurence Llewellyn-Bowen)?
   ❖ Where can you find Morris designs (for example wallpaper, curtains, chairs and tiles)?

✦ Evaluate his designs.
  ❖ Can you see a lot of flowers, plants and animals?
  ❖ Are the designs detailed?
  ❖ Repetitive?
  ❖ Do you like them?
  ❖ What media did he use, do you think?

Activity A

✦ Give each child a postcard-size piece of card; even better, buy postcard blanks for a novelty.

✦ Tell the children to cover the postcard in their own design, in the style of a William Morris print. They could use flowers, petals, leaves etc. This will take some time, as the designs are likely to be quite detailed, so the postcard is a good size to use. Any bigger, and the children may get frustrated or create a design of lesser quality.

✦ Experiment with colours and fill in the design using coloured pencils.

Activity B

✦ Using the postcard designs as a stimulus, explain to the children that they are going to recreate part of their design on a piece of fabric using fabric pens. Follow the manufacturers' guidelines to use the pens. Again, keep the material fairly small, as the patterns will be intricate. I would suggest cutting long rectangles of approximately 6cm x 20cm. The finished result could then be used as a bookmark.

Activity C

You will need: fabric paints; large sheet of material; brushes.

✦ Create a stencil, using a cardboard square or rectangle. You can follow the instructions in the Printing section of this book for this (see activity 76).

✦ Make the stencil in the style of William Morris, choosing just one leaf or petal shape for example.

✦ Let the children work in small groups to print a repeated pattern on a sheet of fabric, the size of a towel, for example. Each child will use their own stencil several times to create part of the pattern. This requires teamwork, so children may need planning time to experiment with rough patterns first.

✦ Children may use the finished results as wallpaper or table covers to be real interior designers of the classroom.

71. **Marbling-ink prints**

You will need: marbling inks; tray; A4 paper.

✦ Children are always fascinated by the patterns created using marbling inks, whatever their age! Marbling inks can be purchased on-line or from most art supplies shops.

✦ Put a few drops of the inks into a plastic tray filled with about 2cm of cold water.

✦ Swirl the inks around so that they intermingle to mix colours.

✦ Lay a piece of paper on top of the water, then remove and leave to dry.

✦ The patterns can be left as they are for display. They can also make a nice background for writing, or can be cut into shapes to link with a mathematics project. Alternatively, you could make up a creative/abstract collage by cutting them up in various ways, or cut them into egg shapes to make Easter cards – there are lots of possibilities!

72. **Christmas wrapping paper**

You will need: silver/gold paints; a variety of ink stampers (eg stars, moons, holly); brown parcel paper.

✦ Get the children to make their own wrapping paper. First, show them some pieces of commercially manufactured wrapping paper and discuss patterns. Are the prints repeated or random?

✦ They can then experiment with some rough designs in pencil or on the computer, using repeated patterns if they wish.

✦ Next, use the stamps to print onto the brown parcel paper.

✦ Use your wrapping paper together with some gold or silver ribbon to wrap a present for a friend or family member.

73. Greetings card

You will need: A4 cardboard in a variety of colours; paints, modelling clay; papers of varying textures/colours or handmade papers; scrap paper; PVA glue.

✦ The children are going to make their own stamper using modelling clay.

✦ First, make a small handle as shown:

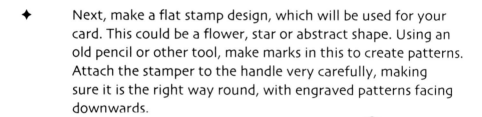

✦ Next, make a flat stamp design, which will be used for your card. This could be a flower, star or abstract shape. Using an old pencil or other tool, make marks in this to create patterns. Attach the stamper to the handle very carefully, making sure it is the right way round, with engraved patterns facing downwards.

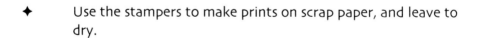

✦ Use the stampers to make prints on scrap paper, and leave to dry.

✦ Cut out one or two of the best prints, and stick them onto a piece of textured or handmade paper.

✦ Stick this onto your A4 card, which has been folded in half to create a greetings card. Shades or contrasting colours can be used for more effect!

74. **Polystyrene prints – candles**

You will need: polystyrene; printing inks; rollers; trays or boards; pencils; paper; art aprons.

✦　Wear art aprons, as inks can be messy!

✦　Cut the polystyrene sheets into tall rectangles, approximately 12cm x 7cm. You will need one for each child.

✦　Next, very faintly sketch a candle in pencil onto your polystyrene, but do not press hard enough to indent.

✦　Then, very carefully, not to go right through the polystyrene, put in dots all along the pencil line as closely together as you can, using a pencil. The pencil just needs to indent the polystyrene, but not go through.

✦　Put ink, the colour of your choice, into a rolling tray and roll it until it makes a 'sticky' noise.

✦　Roll the inked-up roller over your polystyrene block, covering the whole thing.

✦　Place the block onto paper, making a print.

✦　For two colours, simply roll part of the block in one colour and another part in a different colour. Yellows and oranges work especially well for candles.

✦　Experiment with several prints on your sheet. If the design has not come out well, you may have too much ink on the block.

✦　When the prints are dry, select your best ones and cut them out. You can then make a greetings card for Christmas or Diwali, for example, or you could make a collaborative candle border for a hall or corridor.

75. **Tiles**

You will need: pictures of patterned tiles from various cultures; polystyrene; printing inks; rollers; trays or boards; pencils; paper.

✦ Show the children pictures of patterned tiles from various cultures. This could be a great link to other curricular areas. For example: Islamic tiles (RE), Roman tiles (History), geometric tiles (Mathematics) and Mexican tiles (Geography). Discuss.

✦ On a piece of paper 10cm square, design your own patterned tile.

✦ Recreate this design onto a 10cm-square polystyrene block. Use the same method as in the previous activity, using dots to indent the polystyrene block.

✦ Cover your block in inks and print your tiles onto paper. You could use limited colours or contrasting colours for more effect.

✦ Cut, collage and display your tile prints!

76. **Letter prints**

You will need: cardboard; scissors; inks or paint.

✦ The children are going to make a printer using the initial of their first name.

✦ First, design this in pencil on scrap paper 10cm x 10cm. The important things to remember are:

   ❖ The initial must be a capital and in most cases reversed so that it will come out the correct way when printed.

   ❖ The printer will need to be cut from the inside, so that no edges are cut.

   ❖ Leave a slight border around the sides to make the printer stronger.

✦ Check the paper printers, and then ask the children to make the printers using the cardboard.

✦ Use printing inks or paints to cover the printer, then print onto paper. Experiment with colours and backing papers.

✦ Try rotating or repeating the prints to produce a pattern in the style of Andy Warhol. This is very effective.

77. **Big abstract prints**

(Idea inspired by Louis Strachan)

You will need: masking tape; paints; large pieces of sugar paper; various bits and pieces to print with (building-block pieces, cotton reels, bolts, cogs, empty matchboxes and cylinders).

✦ Stick a large piece of sugar paper to a table surface using the masking tape. Place several pieces of tape around the paper to keep it firmly attached and also to create a border around the paper when it is removed. Do not use transparent sticky tape, as this will rip the paper. Masking tape does not.

✦ Get groups of children to print with anything they like, and whatever colour they like, to cover the whole sheet.

✦ Prints can overlap each other; you can have prints on prints.

✦ Overlap some of the prints onto the masking tape. This will make a better effect when the tape is removed, as it will create an edge.

✦ Experiment with colours, shades, and black and white to produce different effects.

78. **String prints**

You will need: thick cardboard; string; PVA glue; paints or printing inks; brushes or rollers.

✦ Stick string onto cardboard squares approximately 10cm x 10cm.

✦ Create patterns with spirally, winding and straight lines.

✦ Use lots of PVA glue, so the string is firmly attached. PVA dries transparent so it won't matter if glue covers the top of the string.

✦ When the string is dry and firmly secured, use paints or inks to cover the string.

✦ Use as a printing block to make wrapping paper, abstract patterns and greeting cards. These prints could also be collaged onto a big shape to make a collaborative print.

79. **Monoprints**

Activity A

You will need: plastic sheet or Perspex sheets; printing-ink; rollers; paper; pencils.

✦ Squeeze some ink of your choice onto the plastic sheet or Perspex and roller over it to cover the entire surface.

✦ Place the sheet of paper on top and smooth it lightly using a ball of scrunched-up kitchen roll, so that it is lying on the sheet or Perspex with ink covering the whole surface.

✦ Draw a design onto the paper. Be careful not to lean on the paper with your hands or fingers, as this will leave a mark too.

✦ Experiment with pressing lightly or harder, drawing thick lines or thinner ones.

✦ Remove the paper to reveal your printed design on the reverse side.

Activity B

You will need: plastic sheet or Perspex sheets; printing-ink; rollers; paper; pencils.

✦ Squeeze ink onto your plastic sheet or Perspex and roller out as before so that the surface is covered.

✦ This time, make marks directly onto the ink, using pencils or other objects like tubes and building bricks.

✦ Place the paper onto the inked surface and dab carefully with a scrunched-up ball of kitchen roll. Do not press hard, but make sure you have pressed gently over all the paper.

✦ Remove the paper to reveal your print design.

Activity C

You will need: plastic sheet or Perspex sheets; printing-ink in a variety of colours; rollers; paper; pencils.

✦ You can repeat either of the previous activities, but this time try using more colours. Simply roller part of the plastic sheet or Perspex with one coloured ink and then another part with a different colour, before making any marks. Place the paper on the ink and follow instructions from either Activity A or B.

80. **Veggie prints**
You will need: chopped-up vegetables; paper; inks or paints.

✦ Printing with vegetables is often associated with young children, but older children still enjoy this too, especially if you prepare some vegetables and cut extra patterns within them so more intricate designs are produced. This needs adult supervision – take care with children using any sort of knife!

✦ Also, instead of printing at random on a big piece of paper, set the older children more of a challenge, for example:

❖ Cut out some giant paper vegetables for the children to print, then display for a Harvest or Thanksgiving Festival.

❖ Get the children to make a picture frame from cardboard, paint it and, once dry, overprint using the vegetables.

❖ Cover a small box with paper, then decorate with veggie prints and fill with a gift.

❖ Make some giant lower-case letters, decorate with veggie prints, then play a game with the Reception class, seeing if they can sound out the letters for you, or make big numbers for them to put in an ordered line.

❖ Cut out large 2D shapes from paper and decorate with veggie prints. Make up a 'Name the Shape' game for the younger children.

❖ Cut out a big Christmas tree, and use the veggie prints to cover it in shades of green. You could add on the prints of candles (see activity 74) you may have made earlier.

✦ Make a figure of your head teacher in paper and decorate with veggie prints. This could look great stuck onto his/her office door!

✦ Make up a collage of a scene or fictional character from a book to go in a reading corner or library.

81. **Black and white prints**

You will need: black and white inks or paints; white and black paper; backing paper; pencils; rulers.

✦ Give the children a square piece of backing paper, 20cm x 20cm.

✦ Divide this into quarters using a pencil and ruler.

✦ Put this aside for later. Next, produce four printed squares 10cm x 10cm to be stuck onto the backing sheet. Two of these squares will be using white ink or paint on black paper; the other two will be using black ink or paint on white paper.

✦ The children must also use four different methods of printing from the knowledge gained from previous activities. For example, they could choose: a monoprint, a string print, a modelling-clay print or a stencil print.

✦ This may take some time, but it is a great challenge for children of this age group and they produce some amazing results.

✦ Once they have produced their four printed squares, they then, may stick them onto the backing sheet to create a wonderful black and white display!

82. **Printing on fabric**

You will need: fabric paints; white or cream fabrics; various printing tools.

✦ The children can try out their printing knowledge from this section using fabric paints and printing on material for a change. Follow instructions as stated on the fabric paints.

✦ Start by using a piece of material, approximately 30cm x 30cm, with which to experiment randomly.

83. **T-shirt print**

You will need: fabric paints; white T-shirts; various printing tools; thick card or newspaper.

✦ Children could then go on to create a design to be printed onto a white T-shirt. When doing this, make sure you have a piece of thick cardboard or a newspaper inside the shirt to prevent the paints going through to the back.

84. Table cover

You will need: fabric paints; old white sheet; various printing tools.

✦ An old white sheet could be collaboratively decorated and used as either a table cover for a display or a wall hanging.

85. Flower print

You will need: fabric paints; white or cream fabrics; round sponge or cardboard tube; various printing tools; modelling clay (optional); green leaves (with lots of veins).

✦ A flower is fairly straightforward to print onto fabric. The children need to start with a circular print, using a round sponge, or cardboard tube, for example.

✦ Next, they need to print around the circle to create individual petals. Again, sponges could be cut to petal shapes or a modelling-clay stamp created.

✦ Leaf prints can be made using real leaves. Choose ones that have lots of veins if possible and ones that are green rather than dried.

86. **Circle scene**

You will need: cardboard or sugar-paper circle (approximately 30cm diameter) for each child; printing inks; paints; various printing tools.

✦ Show the children the circles. Explain to them that they are going to create a scene of their choice using the circle in some way; for example, they may see the circle as a porthole from a ship, a view through a telescope or a fishbowl. Brainstorm ideas of what they see in their minds.

✦ Next, tell them that they are going to cover the whole circle, but that they are allowed to use only printing methods. They may print on separate pieces of paper and stick these on to make up their scenes. For example, they could sponge-print the sea or the sky directly onto the circle, let that dry and then stick on a tropical island and palm tree that they have printed separately using a stencil, or they could print goldfish on fabrics to stick onto their bowl, and add some plants or bubbles created using another method of printing. Point out that they will find it much easier to do the backgrounds first!

✦ You could display the circles with some writing underneath about their scenes to add a link to a literacy session!

87. Alien design

You will need: paper; various printing tools; paints; glue; collage materials.

✦ In a preceding literacy lesson, get the children to describe an alien of their own creation using as many adjectives, adverbs and colours as they can.

✦ Children can then use their printing skills to create printed pictures of their aliens. They could also add collage materials to their aliens to give a mixed-media picture.

88. **Tropical fish**

You will need: thin cardboard; PVA glue; collage materials; pencils; stapler; sticky tape; newspaper; pictures of tropical fish.

✦ Show the children some pictures of tropical fish – the more colourful and patterned the better! Discuss colours, shapes, patterns and textures.

✦ Tell them they are going to create their own tropical fish. First they need to draw a fish on the card, leaving the mouth big enough to push newspaper into later.

✦ Cut out two fish by having a second piece of card underneath the first. Stick them together, putting glue only around the inner edges (or staple) and leaving the mouth open.

✦ Fill the fish with some newspaper so it becomes 3D, then glue the mouth so that the newspaper filling is sealed inside.

✦ Have fun decorating your fish with whatever collage materials you have found. PVA glue works better than glue sticks if using scraps of fabric. Fins can be stapled or taped on for more security if you find the glue doesn't hold. Try to decorate the entire fish.

✦ Hang the tropical fish from the ceiling by attaching string to the fishes' backs. They look great when they move around in the breeze!

89. Snow scene

You will need: thick cardboard; collage materials in shades of cream; silver and white; glue; fabrics in shades of cream and white.

✦ The children are going to make a snow scene using limited colour for effect. By using varying materials – eg net curtain, papers, wool and sequins – even the white will vary hugely in appearance.

✦ They may choose to do a landscape, or a snowman or a tree covered in snow. Brainstorm some ideas and write them on to a board.

✦ First they need to cut a piece of fabric about 3cm larger all round than the piece of cardboard.

✦ Cover the cardboard with fabric, taping or gluing it to the back of the cardboard. This will act as the baseboard for their snow scene.

✦ Then cut out pieces of paper, card, fabric etc and stick them on the baseboard to make the scene. A good tip is to do most of the cutting first and experiment by placing all the pieces on the board, and then stick them down when you are happy with the finished article.

✦ Let the children experiment with all sorts of textures, but do NOT let them be tempted to add in any other colours. By using white, creams and silvers, you will have a very effective product, and one in which the quality is lifted, in comparison to scenes made previously perhaps, lower down the school, when they used any colours they liked.

90. African masks

You will need: thin cardboard; PVA glue; assorted materials for collage (eg dried lentils, split peas, rice, grains, string, small feathers, sand); pencils; pictures of African masks and (ideally) some real African masks; pre-cut square blocks of wood (optional).

✦ Show the children the masks and pictures of masks, and discuss what they see in terms of shape, colour, texture, pattern and materials. Where have they been made? What makes the masks look African? Write the children's ideas on a board.

✦ Tell the children they are going to make an African mask using various materials.

✦ First they need to fold their cardboard in half with the fold vertically central. Then they will draw half a mask along the folded side, so when they cut it out, it will unfold and be symmetrical.

✦ Next they must cover the whole mask in the above-mentioned collage materials so that all the mask is decorated and no cardboard can be seen. This decorating does not need to be symmetrical. Be generous with the glue. PVA glue dries clear, so they will not end up with white blobs everywhere!

✦ When the masks are dry, mount them onto the blocks of wood by stapling the masks to two of the sides (best done by an adult using a staple gun!). These allow the masks to stand and be displayed on a table.

91. **Sunset strips**

You will need: tissue paper in various shades of red, orange and yellow; pots of water; brushes; black sugar paper; glue; A3 or A4 white paper.

✦ Tear up strips of tissue paper and place them onto the white paper so that they join or even overlap slightly. Use different-coloured strips each time so no two the same are placed next to each other.

✦ Using a brush, paint over them with water so the tissue paper gets wet and the strips stick to the paper. Do not use glue!

✦ When the water has dried, peel off the tissue-paper strips and discard. The colours released from the tissue-paper strips should have run onto the paper and blended into each other. If there are any gaps of white paper showing through, use the brush and water to cover them, as the colours should still run slightly.

✦ Once your background is dry, cut out a scene using the black sugar paper and stick it onto the background, forming silhouettes against your sunset strip. The children may come up with anything they like (trees, buildings, people or animals), or they may choose an object such as a chair or electric guitar to make a more abstract creation.

92. **Natural-material collages**

You will need: cardboard, PVA glue; lots of natural materials, eg leaves, flowers (not precious wild ones!); wool; feathers; sand; thin twigs; grasses and dried pulses or grains; pencils or a colouring medium of your choice.

✦ Cut the cardboard into a big circle, just as a change from using a rectangular background.

✦ Next, draw any natural object as large as you can to fit the space (a flower, a tree, an insect, a sea horse, an elephant). Keep this a simple sketch, because it needs only to be a guide for collage.

✦ Cover the whole object with natural materials, sticking them on with generous amounts of PVA glue. The smaller the pieces, the more effective the collage, so don't be afraid of cutting up your feather or twig into little pieces. Leave the background free.

✦ Once the collage is dry, colour in your background using media and colours of your choice.

93. **Bedroom design**

You will need: catalogues to cut up/pictures of bedroom furniture; A3 paper; wallpapers; glue; coloured pencils or pens.

✦   The children are going to design their ideal bedroom on A3 paper.

✦   First, give them time to browse pictures and cut out beds, sets of drawers and televisions.

✦   Then get them to place their favourites onto the A3 paper. When they are happy with the layout, they may stick on some wallpaper, or paper to form a carpet, and stick down these objects on top.

✦   Use the coloured pencils or pens at the end to add optional extras such as a lampshade or a favourite teddy.

94. **Symmetry in contrast**

You will need: A4 and A5 sugar paper in red, yellow, blue, green, orange and purple; scissors; glue.

✦   Revise the idea of contrasting colours from your Contrasting Colour Wheel (activity 39).

✦   Choose two contrasting colours (eg red and green).

✦   Take an A4 piece of green paper and an A5 piece of red (or vice versa).

✦   Cut out lots of shapes from the A5 piece and lay them on the left side of the A4 sheet. Do not cut into the A5 sheet, as it will be used in the design too; instead, fold the paper to cut out the shapes rather than cutting from the side inwards.

✦   Stick the A5 sheet onto the right side of the A4 sheet and glue all the cut-out pieces so that they are symmetrical to the spaces made in the smaller sheet.

✦   You should end up with a symmetrical pattern in contrasting colours. Again, double-back the work on red then green (or on whatever your two colours) paper to add to the effect.

95. **Mosaic spirals**

You will need: coloured paper (cut into approximately 1cm squares); A3 paper; pencils; glue.

✦ This is a nice link to learning about Roman mosaics in history. It is a simple yet effective activity.

✦ Draw a spiral onto your A3 paper as circular as you can, and making the space in-between the lines about 1cm.

✦ Start in the middle of the spiral, sticking on your 1cm squares of coloured paper and work your way around the spiral line, leaving as little space as possible between squares.

✦ Limited colours, shades or contrasting colours could be used to create more effective patterns.

✦ Make sure the final circuit of the spiral is done using just one dark colour, eg black, navy blue, dark green, as this will give the spiral an outline, making it more outstanding.

✦ Once the spirals are complete, display them along your classroom wall or in a corridor!

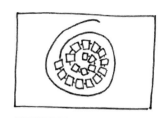

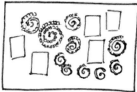

96. **Recycled messages**

You will need: A4 thin card; glue; scissors; recycled materials (eg papers, sweet wrappers, newspaper, some plastics, clean food wrappings, labels from jars or tins, or cardboard).

✦ Bring in lots of materials that usually end up in the bin. These need to be clean and fairly flat so that they can be stuck onto card.

✦ Decide on a slogan or message that may link to a recycling or environmental topic, for example:

> RECYCLE TO HELP THE PLANET
> SAVE THE ENVIRONMENT AND RECYCLE
> DON'T DROP LITTER AROUND OUR SCHOOL!

✦ Allocate one letter to each child, and get them to draw this on their A4 card. Choose if you want upper- or lower-case letters, bubble writing or a mixture of styles and fonts. Decide if you want them all to be approximately the same height, eg 30cm.

✦ Next, cut out pieces from the materials brought in and stick them all over the letter at random, making sure the card is totally covered.

✦ Cut out the letters and put up your message!

97. **Papier mâché faces**

You will need: balloons; PVA glue or flour and water mix; paints; brushes; wool; collage materials; newspaper.

✦ Blow up some balloons and cover each one in about three layers of papier mâché. The key to successful papier mâché is to keep the pieces of newspaper small. Use watered-down PVA glue or a mix of flour and water as your gluing medium. I love the flour mix as it is nice on the skin and it smells gorgeous! Soak the newspaper in the mix and lay onto the balloon, overlapping as you go. The children can do this in pairs.

✦ Let the papier mâché dry, then cut the balloon shape in half lengthways, removing the old balloon at the same time.

✦ Each child will then decorate their balloon half, making it into a face. They can paint it first, then add on other features with collage scraps and PVA glue. Wool makes great hair, for example.

✦ If you intend to display these faces on a wall, it is a good tip to attach a loop of ribbon or string to the back of them during the papier mâché stage. This will enable you to hang them with more ease later.

✦ Perhaps you could write play scripts, using the faces as masks, to add a link to a literacy session.

98. **Balloon monsters**

You will need: PVA glue or flour and water mix; balloons; wool; newspaper; paints; brushes; additional scrap cardboard.

✦ Give each child a balloon, blow it up and cover it in the same way as in the previous activity.

✦ Cut out some hands and feet from thin card and join these to the balloon using masking tape or papier mâché. Cover these monster limbs in newspaper too.

✦ Leave to dry, remove the balloons and then paint the monsters using some bright, funky colours.

✦ Write a story about your 3D monster to link to literacy work!

99. **Picture frames**

You will need: PVA glue or flour and water mix; paints, brushes; newspaper; ribbon; cardboard frame; lentils, rice and/or dried peas.

✦ Each child needs to cut a frame out of cardboard. You can make it any size you like. This is a great link to measuring in mathematical work.

✦ Cover the frame in papier mâché as in the previous activities, and add in the lentils, rice, dried peas etc on the last layer to give the frame different textures. Use PVA glue to make sure these are firmly secured.

✦ Let the frames dry thoroughly, then paint them as you choose.

✦ When the paint is dry, paint a final layer of PVA glue over the entire frame. It will dry clear and add a slight shine to your frames.

✦ Make a loop out of ribbon to attach to the back of the frame.

✦ Use your frames to display a piece of work from other curricular areas or a piece of artwork.

100. **Gift boxes**

You will need: PVA glue or flour and water mix; newspaper; collage materials (pulses, pasta, wools, string etc); paint; brushes; ribbon; cardboard boxes (approximately the size of a tea-bag box).

◆   Cover a box with papier mâché.

◆   Experiment with texture by adding pulses, pasta, wools and string onto your final layer.

◆   Leave to dry, then paint. When dry, add a final layer of PVA glue, as in the previous activity.

◆   Once dry, fill the box with a layer of tissue paper.

◆   Your box is now ready to be used as a gift box for a friend or family member.

101. **Tonal collage**

You will need: A3 or A4 thin card (black, white or grey); various papers (black, white, grey); PVA glue.

✦ The aim of this activity is to experiment with lots of different textures of paper, and to focus on the tonal shades of black, grey, white – colours more often associated with shading in drawing but overlooked in other areas of art media.

✦ The children are to make their own pattern, collaging pieces of paper onto a background sheet.

✦ Encourage them to be adventurous with the paper. For example, instead of laying paper flat onto the background, why not stick folded pieces onto it? Other ways to use paper could be making spirals, cutting fringes, making straight lines in various widths, layering paper so that it builds upwards etc. Use the paper pieces in as many different ways as you can.

✦ At the end, ask volunteers to discuss their patterns giving self-evaluation, eg what they did, what they liked, did not like so much, what was successful, what they thought about using limited tones, etc.

102. **Making shakers**

You will need: tubes or boxes; dried pulses; pasta; glue; collage materials; elastic bands; masking tape.

✦ Choose a tube or a small box. Fill it with some pulses or pasta and seal the open ends with paper and masking tape or elastic bands, making sure no pulses/pasta are going to come out.

✦ Decorate your shakers with paper and collage materials, and add paint if you wish.

✦ Use your shakers in a music lesson to compose your own piece of music, or have fun joining in with your friends making up rhythm patterns.

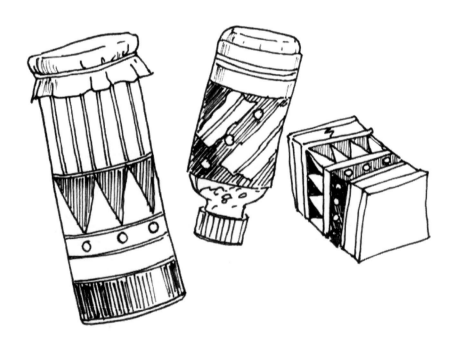

103. Matisse-style collage

You will need: pictures by Henri Matisse; paper; collage materials; glue; scissors.

✦ Show the children lots of pictures by artist Henri Matisse (1869-1954). Matisse was a famous painter and sculptor, known for creating patterns, scenes and art depicting the human form. These pictures will act as a stimulus for this collage activity.

✦ Discuss the pictures with the children. Which pictures do the children like and why? Do they prefer his patterns or scenes? Are there any common threads in his style? How does he show the human body? What colours does he use?

✦ The children are going to make their own collage in the style of Matisse. Some children may like to experiment with pattern; others may like to create a human figure. Let them choose.

✦ At the end of the session, ask some volunteers to evaluate their work, and then make a 'Matisse' display.

✦ Other artists' work can be used in exactly the same way. A collaborative collage could be made based on a scene by Lowry for example.

104. General collage ideas

Collage can be used in so many ways and can create lovely links to other curricular areas, some of which I am going to list below. A top tip is that the key to creating a realistic scene using collage is to use small pieces, as the end result will be neater. Always use pictures by artists or photographs to stimulate each activity if possible.

◆ Collage a building. You could take inspiration from a Tudor house, Hindu temple or local building.

◆ Collage a landscape, townscape or water scene.

◆ Collage a face, portrait or a full-size figure.

◆ Collage a vase of flowers, bowl of fruit or other still life.

◆ Collage an animal, tree or plant.

◆ Collage a scene from history (for example, you could use images of London during the Blitz).

◆ Collage a geographical feature, such as a volcano.

◆ Collage a sporting scene or figure.

◆ Make an abstract collage with a scientific theme, such as electricity or light.

◆ Collage geometric shapes, rotational shapes or symmetrical patterns as a link to mathematics.

◆ Collage a 'Healthy Eating' or 'Look After Your Teeth' poster.

105. Withy tipis
You will need: pictures of Native American tipis; withies (long, bendy willow sticks); masking tape; tissue paper; PVA glue; scissors.

✦ You can buy withies online. Make sure you soak them overnight in a bath so that they are supple to use.

✦ Show the children some pictures of Native American tipis and discuss. How were they made? What was used? Do they have any patterns or designs on them?

✦ Give each group of children some withies, which they can cut to the required length (approximately 30cm). Get them to join the withies together using the masking tape to form a tipi shape.

✦ Next, glue tissue paper onto the withies and let everything dry. Tissue paper is light; heavier materials can make the structure collapse.

✦ Add Native American designs using felt-tipped pens and pastels.

106. Withy mini-beasts
You will need: pictures of mini-beasts; withies (long, bendy willow sticks); masking tape; tissue paper; PVA glue; scissors; pipe cleaners (optional).

✦ Again, work in small groups and use the withies and masking tape to create a mini-beast such as a fly, butterfly, bee, wasp or dragonfly.

✦ Use tissue paper to decorate. Again, don't be tempted to use heavier materials, as the structures may collapse. Pipe cleaners could be used for smaller features such as antennae.

✦ Withies may be used in a similar way to make sea creatures, dragons or other animals.

107. **Rolled-up-newspaper hats**

You will need: lots of newspaper; masking tape; paints; collage materials; glue; scissors; PVA glue or flour (optional).

✦ Challenge your children to make a hat using rolled-up tubes of newspaper and masking tape only. The rolls of paper can be bent, and are surprisingly versatile. The more sheets of paper you have in your roll, the sturdier the structure. Single-sheet rolls can be used for more intricate details (these can also be cut to the required length).

✦ Children will need to measure their heads, think about a structure that will not collapse once worn and also think about the attractive nature of their hats.

✦ Once the hat structure is complete, the children can paint them or add collage materials. Be careful not to soak the newspaper when painting or the hat may fall apart. Use thick paints (you could add PVA glue or flour to thicken).

✦ Other ideas for rolled-up newspaper and masking tape: spiders, animals and bridges all work well.

Art Activities

108. Art-straw tower challenge

You will need: art straws; masking tape; some small wooden building blocks; large picture of the Eiffel Tower.

✦ Give each group of children the same amount of masking tape and art straws.

✦ Challenge them to make the tallest tower they can in an allotted time. The tower must hold the weight of three wooden building blocks (or one if you have only large ones).

✦ Evaluate which tower is the strongest and why. Is the tallest also the strongest?

✦ Look at how the children have made their structure. Has anybody used triangles in their structure?

✦ Finally, show the group a poster of the Eiffel Tower and discuss its design.

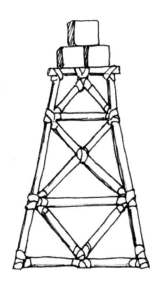

109. Celtic jewellery

You will need: clay; clay tools; pictures of Celtic patterns; string; paint (optional); PVA glue (optional).

✦ Show the children the Celtic pattern designs and discuss. Who were the Celts? Do you think they wore jewellery? How was it made? Where would they find clay? How did they come up with these designs?

✦ In their sketch or ideas books, get the children to design a pendant with a Celtic design on it. This can be any shape but needs to be about 6cm in length. Don't make it too small, as it may not be strong enough; too big, and it will be too heavy to wear.

✦ Next, give each child some clay. Work it until it is malleable. Roll it to about 1.5cm thickness. Cut out your pendant shape.

✦ Put a hole through the pendant using a pencil, but not too close to the edge or the clay will not hold the weight once dry. The hole needs to be wide enough to thread string through it.

✦ Add your Celtic design using various tools or a pencil.

✦ Once dry, thread with string. You may paint the pendants or simply give them a layer of PVA glue for shine. Remember PVA will dry clear.

110. Art-deco tiles

You will need: pictures of art-deco tiles; clay; clay tools; thin card; pencils; rulers; paint; PVA glue or clay varnish.

✦ Art deco was a style popular between the two World Wars. It was greatly influenced and inspired by the archaeological finds in Egypt during the 1920s. Geometric patterns together with bold glossy colours (and black) are typically seen in art-deco designs.

✦ Show the children your pictures and discuss the age of, and inspiration behind the designs. Evaluate the patterns and colours on the tiles. Where might you find tiles like these in a house between the two World Wars (eg floor tiles, fireside tiles, kitchen tiles)?

✦ Give each child a cardboard square approximately 12cm x 12cm, on which to draw their rough design in pencil, a design in the art-deco tradition. Get them to think about the colours they wish to use later.

✦ Roll the clay out like pastry to no less than 1cm thick. Place the cardboard square on top and cut out a square of clay using clay tools.

✦ Put your art-deco design onto the clay tile using pencils, rulers and tools.

✦ Once dry, paint the tiles in bright colours and try to use black in the design somewhere too.

✦ Go over the dry paint with a clay varnish or PVA glue to get the glossy effect.

✦ Display your tiles for the rest of the school to see!

111. **Thumb pots**

You will need: clay; paints (optional); PVA glue (optional).

✦ This is a simple activity for all ages. Give each child some clay to work into a ball shape. Work the clay until it is malleable.

✦ Carefully place your thumb into the centre of the ball until it reaches about three-quarters down. Do not go right through to the bottom, or this will break or weaken your pot.

✦ Using your thumb, work the clay so that the hole becomes larger and a pot is formed.

✦ Smooth the sides and flatten the bottom slightly so that the pot stands up on its own.

✦ When dry, paint the pots or give them a layer of PVA glue for shine, or both.

112. Coil pots

You will need: clay; paints (optional); clay tools; pencils; PVA glue or clay varnish (optional).

✦ Cut out a circle or square from the clay, no less than 1cm thick. Use this as your base.

✦ Roll out long sausage or worm shapes from the clay, about 1cm in diameter.

✦ Carefully coil these around the base of the pot, overlapping them to build up the walls.

✦ Dip your fingers into water and use this to smooth the clay side and the base so that the coils are firmly attached.

✦ If you began with a circular base, you should end up with a round pot. If you had a square base, you will end up with a cube or cuboid shape.

✦ Older or more able children can use clay tools or pencils to indent decorative designs into the pots.

✦ When the clay is dry, you can paint or add a varnish as required.

113. Clay heads

You will need: clay; pictures of heads sculpted by other artists (or real artefacts); clay tools; old garlic crusher or pasta machine (optional); PVA glue.

✦ Show the children the pictures/artefacts and discuss them; these may include African heads or religious ones (Buddha heads are relatively popular). You may link this to a geography, history or RE lesson. If doing Buddha heads or any other religious icon, make sure this is not going to offend any parents/carers who may disagree with the concept.

✦ Give each child some clay and get them to work on making a head. The head will need to stand on its own, so make them aware of this at the beginning.

✦ Children will tend to make features and push them onto the main head. They then get upset when the clay is dry and the features fall off. The way to avoid this is to use 'slip'. Make a mini thumb pot and put some water in it, then swirl it round with your finger so that it becomes a mixture of water and clay. Use this 'slip' mixture as glue for sticking on your features. If an ear is stuck on well and smoothed with 'slip', it should remain on when the clay dries!

✦ Use clay tools to add more designs or features. Children love making hair by pushing clay through a garlic crusher or an old pasta machine.

✦ When the heads are dry, add a layer of PVA glue to give a glossy finish.

114. Pencil pot holder

You will need: cardboard; collage materials; masking tape; optional paints; glue.

✦ Bring in a pencil pot holder or desk tidy, if you can, and show this to the children. What can it hold? Ruler? Pencils? Small objects such as erasers or drawing pins? Discuss its colour, and what it was made from.

✦ Get the children to spend 10 minutes making rough sketches of a pencil pot-holder design in their sketch/ideas books.

✦ The children are going to need a thick cardboard base and then thinner cardboard to make tubes or cylinders of various widths and lengths.

✦ By making 2cm cuts around the base of the tubes, they can fan out small sections that can be attached to the base with masking tape.

✦ Make sure all cylinders are attached firmly, then decorate with papers, collage materials or paints. Use thick paints so that the cardboard does not get too wet and collapse.

✦ Use your new pencil pot holder on your desk at home!

115. **Treasure island**

You will need: wooden board for a base; wire mesh; masking tape; newspaper; paints; wall stapler (for use by adults); PVA glue or flour and water mix; paint.

✦ Work in groups. First, make a rough design for your ideal treasure island on paper. Will it have hills? A cave? A river? Sandy beaches? Waterfalls? Volcanos?

✦ Use the wooden board as a base and make the island out of pieces of bent wire netting and/or rolled-up newspaper. Attach these with masking tape. If the wire needs firmer attachment, an adult could add some staples using a wall stapler (not for use by the children!).

✦ Cover the whole thing with about four layers of papier mâché (see activity 97).

✦ Once dry, make additional objects for your island. You could make walls and bridges.

✦ Have fun painting your islands.

✦ Once finished, evaluate the islands and discuss what the children enjoyed about making them.

✦ You could then link this activity to literacy or geography by doing some writing to display with them.

116. **2D robots**

You will need: pictures of robots; thick backing paper or card; glue; shiny collage materials.

✦ Look at the robot pictures and discuss what the children like or dislike about them.

✦ Tell your children that they are going to make a 2D robot using various collage materials, but they are allowed to use only squares or rectangles to do this. Even the eyes and ears must be made out of these shapes too.

✦ They can stick more squares/rectangles on top of base ones to make the robot more detailed.

✦ Perhaps they could then draw a background for their robot and colour it using shades of one colour as an extra challenge!

117. **3D robots**

You will need: lots of boxes of varying sizes; paper, glue; collage materials; masking tape; glue gun (optional - under adult supervision); paint.

◆ This is based on activity 116, but this time the robot is made in 3D. Instead of squares and rectangles, the children will make a robot using only cubes and cuboids.

◆ They can work individually or in groups depending on your amount of resources.

◆ Make the robots by taping boxes together with masking tape, as it holds better than glue. Glue guns could be used under adult supervision if you have them.

◆ Decorate or paint your robots, then display them on a table, perhaps near your 2D robots.

◆ You could add some literacy work to this display too. Examples include descriptive writing about robots, a robot story or sets of instructions on 'how to make a 3D robot'.

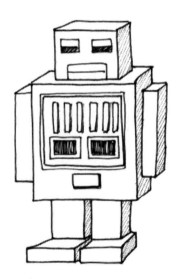

118. **Modroc bowls**

You will need: Modroc; tissue paper; thin coloured fabric; wire mesh; pictures of bowls by various artists; art aprons; newspaper.

✦ Look at the photographs/pictures of bowls made by various artists. Discuss the shapes, sizes, uses and designs of the bowls.

✦ Give each child a piece of wire mesh, approximately 30–40cm squared.

✦ Bend the wire to a bowl shape. This could be deep or shallow, depending on taste.

✦ Once the child is happy with the shape, cover the bowl in Modroc (bandages impregnated with a plaster substance, which, when moistened with water, will stick to the wire). This can be messy, so make sure children wear aprons and you work outside or in an area in the room that is well covered in newspaper.

✦ Before the Modroc has dried out, cover it in pieces of thin fabrics and tissue papers until the bowl is entirely covered, including the inside.

✦ Leave the bowls to dry and then evaluate them with your children.

119. **Modroc flowers**

You will need: Modroc; tissue paper; thin coloured fabric; wire mesh; pipe cleaners.

✦ This activity works in the same way as activity 118. The children are going to make a flower-head shape from the wire mesh.

✦ They may add in the stigma, stamens etc using pipe cleaners or more wire.

✦ Cover the flowers in Modroc pieces and then add tissue paper/ thin fabrics before it has dried out.

✦ This is a good link to science, as you can display the flowers, either labelling each part of the plant or displaying them with written work on the life cycle of a butterfly or flowering plant.

120. **Wire-mesh animals**

You will need: wire mesh; newspaper; glue; Modroc; paints.

✦ Each group of children needs to think of an animal they want to make, eg snake, giraffe or elephant.

✦ First, they need to make the structure using the wire mesh as a frame.

✦ Next, they can cover it in Modroc (or papier mâché, if they prefer).

✦ Once dried, paint the animals and display.

Masks can also be made in this way; figures of people, sea creatures and mini-beasts work well too!

121. Mixed-media collage

You will need: Modroc; paper; fabrics; collage materials; sequins; paint, pictures of abstract works from various artists; thick cardboard for the backing.

✦ Show the children the pictures made by various abstract artists. Discuss.

✦ The children are going to make their own abstract, mixed-media collages, using whatever they choose.

✦ Give them some time to plan what they want to do. Think about colours; perhaps they can use shades, limited colours or contrasting colours, using the knowledge gained from previous sessions.

✦ Make the collages, let them dry, add more to them to make them really intricate and let them dry again.

✦ Evaluate the creations, then make a wonderful abstract display so everyone can see them!

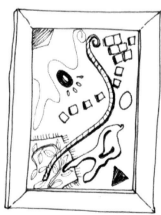

122. **Shadow fish**

You will need: black sugar paper; scissors, pencils; tape; sticks; torches.

✦ This is a nice link to science work on light and shadows. The children are going to make a fish that can be used to produce interesting shadows with the help of a torch beam.

✦ Draw a fish outline on the black sugar paper, approximately A4 size. Do not make the fish too small, or the next stage will be too fiddly!

✦ Cut out intricate patterns inside the fish. The easiest way to do this is to fold parts of the fish over and cut out half a shape. When unfolded, it makes a hole in the paper without needing to cut from the outside inwards, causing the fish to fall apart. (The technique is very similar to making a snowflake from a folded circle.)

✦ Encourage the children to make small cuts, having lots of tiny shapes cut out as opposed to a few big shapes. This will depend on each individual's ability when using scissors.

✦ When the fish is finished, tape a stick to the back of it and have fun shining torches at it or putting it in front of an overhead projector in a darkened room. As a link to literacy, the children could write a shadow play for their fish, or they could extend the technique and create other shadow creatures!

Award Certificate

presented to

_____

on _____

to thank you for your help in tidying up
the classroom.

_____

Art teacher

Art Activities

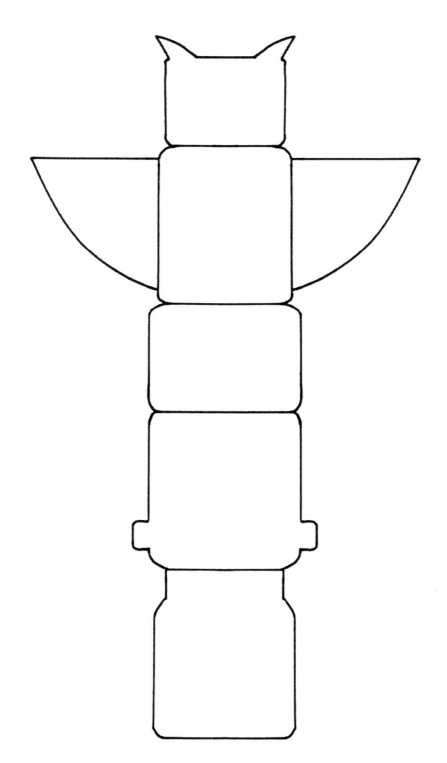

Art Activities

Art Activities

Index

3D and other ideas